– if you're not happy now –

– *if you're not happy now* –

AN ANTHOLOGY

POEMS BY THE BOSTON UNIVERSITY
MFA POETRY CLASS OF 2018

EMILY YAREMCHUK
KATHLEEN RADIGAN
LAUREN PEAT
REBECCA LEVI
ERIC HERTZ
DANIEL HARDISTY
LIBBY GOSS
MADELINE GILMORE

With an afterword by
ROBERT PINSKY

For Nina,
With love and decades
of friendship, music,
gardens!

Broadstone

Library of Congress Control Number 2018966023

ISBN 978-1-937968-53-3

Text Design & Composition by Larry W. Moore
Cover Artwork & Design by Eleanor Birle,
used by permission.

Broadstone Books
An Imprint of
Broadstone Media LLC
418 Ann Street
Frankfort, KY 40601-1929
BroadstoneBooks.com

The poets are so grateful to their professors,
Robert Pinsky, Karl Kirchwey, and Gail Mazur,
for giving us the space and support to write these poems,
and for reminding us that poetry is a communal art.
Thank you to the Boston University
Creative Writing Department, especially Catherine Con.
We carry our year in Room 222 with us.

Contents

POEMS BY DANIEL HARDISTY

POEMS BY LIBBY GOSS

POEM BY MADELINE GILMORE

EMILY YAREMCHUK

Tabula Rasa

When you're late getting home from work,
I sift through your things,
sticking mostly to your shelf in the closet

your knick-knacks, breath mints,
the brass plate with its mouthful of cufflinks
and loose change.

Ever since Uncle Bobby told me that
you really wanted a son, the braille of boyhood
has been upon me. It pricks me all over

when I lift your several pocketknives
and unfold them, slick and silvered,
and heavy as lead butterflies.

I begin to like the sulfur smell
that hangs on the dark. I cannot get
the matches to light.

I'm wild for heirlooms. The cold jacket
of an old bullet fits snug in my cheek.
It is easy to become you among these things.

In the second drawer, I unearth
your marriage license and faded pornography
beneath a phalanx of rolled socks.

I'm your daughter. I can disappear entirely
in a rack of your suits. I cut the daffodils
out front before they are done growing,

fix their waxy stems between my fingers
like puppeteer's bars. I piss in the yard
like I am God.

Now I am twenty-one and the world
is about to receive me. I am a woman,
Uncle Bobby is a drunk. And though you love me,

my heart is a man, grows 5 o'clock shadow,
calls for an armchair and whiskey sour,
slurring, *put a light on and I'll watch.*

Ode to Orchid

I have lost my identity

waking
with her in the room,

on the dresser
plied with light.

A backlit hare's ear—

and winter's white leg
bare to the thigh.

I hear you feed her
ice chips twice a month,

annually break
her roots.

The staunchness of morning
a choking hand

she's grown into.

I have no wicket to lean on,
like the orchid

all neck, lulled and
sleepy-weak.

The poor girl is tied
to a stake for life

with the taste of bonfire
in her cheek.

I admire
her geisha-fan head,

her purpleness
just right.

How she sleeps off desire
while I dream of eating

ice from your hand

the way an orchid
eats light.

Wednesday Night At The Singhs

Tuna is gross, I say.
You're aware,
but the oven and microwave
are taken, filled with
last year's sweaters and
your little sister's pottery.
You slice the bread mournfully.
Outside on the porch, your parents
have their Russian friends over,
scattering cigar ash,
swirling red wine in their glasses
so it runs down the sides:
upturned fire ants.
Wide-eyed above the guttural banter,
the porch light hums a dull opinion
no one is interested in,
and the indignant Persian carpet gasps
through mouthfuls of chest hair:
Are those your names?
Are those your real names?

MONTHLYS

You, listen: I was
that lucky child,
given a Russian doll
for Christmas.

She was fat, a glossy bean,
slap-mark red, her ample chin bound
with blue scarf, cheeks
inflamed apples.

I didn't know what to make of her
until someone told me
you have to open
her to get the point.

I did it with a twist, clipped
her at the waist. She smelled
of juniper varnish,
the air inside her cool

as a palmful of mausoleum. Under the tree
I detonated her daughters one by one,
each blondie more empty than the last,
divulging fresh girlhood

with a sound as clean
as a snapping poker chip.
That day I wore their heads like thimbles
on my hand, wiggled them to chatter,

considered the vacant bottoms,
their hard O's of orifice,
absent of anything, unlike
the male torso in science class,

regal plasticine with his
laurel wreath of intestine,
plait of colon,
purple fist of heart.

The smallest of the dolls was whole
and slight enough to swallow.
She too contained nothing
that could be seen,

her pawn's body a
seed of secret,
not empty
but anonymous.

Beautiful Village

On those January trips to Florida,
my Grandfather told me all kinds of things
he wasn't supposed to.

Why Grandma left,
the right way to say bride price,
what happened to all the Russian poets.

I was five,
I ate ten of his heart pills
because they were blue.

When they found the rest laid out in constellation,
my parents took off my clothes
and fed me a spoonful of clear Ipecac.

In the bathtub, I vomited over the drain,
feeling betrayed,
the green stuff that came up oddly floral

as if made from the crushed stems
of every flower I had ever picked,
my first taste of penitence

and something to be remembered,
like the Russian poets buried
with the ball of their femurs in their mouths.

Kathleen Radigan

Augur

The storm blows down
a hundred-year-old pine
just inches from the house.

Now, out the kitchen
window, my mother looks
over its hulk trunk, lichen-
swollen.

The cancer passed
over, left contrails
on her breasts.

When they noticed,
doctors sank gloved hands
inside her skin.
Pulled out the tumor,
a dove from a hat.

Hear her slippers all night
through the kitchen.

The countertop shines
in the dark like a deer's eye.
She pounds chicken
with murderous force.

Parts meat with a knife
and gut-glossed hands.
Pulls heart from carcass, keeps
a wishbone for after.

Plea to God

Before You knock me up, let me birth fistfuls
of gold moths. Water snakes.
Let ants dance out my mouth.
I'm only fourteen. I haven't felt a lot.
I want sisters who are lizards.
Peer inside my belly full of animals
—a circus, three thousand evolutionary years.
I'll die a good virgin. I'll lick his wounds,
lock my knees, shelter him in spine.

Prophets say he's destined for a salt grave.
I'll water his bones with tears.
But first I want gardens. Moony daughters whose braces
collect sun. A pool of Your saliva as an emblem.

My Mother

Met my father
in summer
at some wedding.
She won't say
if they kissed
or felt clairvoyant
twinges during Vows.
"That's private."

She cracks pistachios,
flings shells out
the car window.
I bet her hair hung
like a waterfall,
cheeks sunburnt.
Green-eyed in the pew.

Kept clean fingernails,
knew her grandmother's
friends by name.
She's like tarot
now, all predictions.
Hides old selves
under starched shirts.
Talks like a bottle rocket.

Radiologists call
from a bright-
ceilinged world
where death and life
are zigzags on a screen.
Can it be true?
Each day is dead so soon.

Eve

Forgive me. I've
eaten your clementines.
Skin of vine,

sinful rot.
I am a rib made mistress.
Seed in my lungs.

Wet rapes.
We are your inmates:
the temptress and the ape.

Tore blooms off
your fruit tree, bored
of bramble and the animals'

scared scuttle.
Forgive me, heart blinking
through my hunger.

They were cold.
With Eden dead,
Adam will eat me soon.

See how he eyes my thighs,
strokes my spine
with a knife.

Calls me the new fruit,
drooling to take
my life.

Happy

The grief I've known
is an almond
in my throat.

Nonna and I drink gin
in an Indian restaurant.
Some of my friends'

parents I say
don't love each other anymore.
She sucks teeth. All these

shotgun weddings.
Say they're in love
after six months.

You can't know
she says who that
person will be.

She says Maybe
after ten fine years
he'll punch you

till your teeth bleed.
You have no idea she says
what heartbreak is and you

have a new boyfriend, good grades –
if you're not happy now,
when will you ever be?

The Kitchen Staff at Oceanworld Bar & Grille

We soak and stack plates,
sponge down knives. Briana
does standing push-ups against
the fridge, dragons etched into
her arms. She's twenty-two,
I'm twenty. We slice pickles
into spears.

She says she would've been
an astronaut but her vision
is shit so it's fine she got
knocked up. I say I'm sad
about a man. She says,
"Men are liars." (Once she found
her friend dead, stabbed
in a bathroom. Three kids
crying in a locked closet.)

She flips patties, smiles side-eyed
at the griddle,
slides me a ham sandwich.
Her girls are 7 and 4.
She boils them hot dogs
after each shift, toasts the buns.
She says they're going
to the public pool tomorrow.
She says, "Don't think
you'll never find someone
because we've all felt
like that and we all found someone."

Then clocks out. Double
doors swish behind her. Soap
bubbles on her T-shirt. Drowning
she swims with a riptide. Spat up
from the ocean.

Lauren Peat

Postscript

On the first day I acquainted my clothes,
my books, my cardboard excuses for belongings
with the battered planks of your front porch,
and with four hands we admitted them
two by two. On the second day I FaceTimed Sara
(who always asks first *How was your day*?)
and across the sea spray of static I said
It was good—look at this hardwood, this cactus,
this new life. On the fourth day we seeded
the last of the IKEA screws, and on the fifth grew
fat with pride: over the disassembled flesh
of soppy peaches we went through the foods
you didn't like, plants I wouldn't water, things
that made the other's neck hair stand on end.
(We were visionary, we moved quickly.)

On the seventh day you had no mind for rest,
as our island was beginning to take back
its tendrils and fend for its very own—
you were tracking down cat food at Costco
when mammals started dropping small misgivings
in large print across the ground. I had no sound
to describe the way your face would fall
when this disproved you, so I silently ate
a creature we called *crow* when all I'd done
was neglect to fetch a broom in time.

On the eighth day you stayed but left me
behind, and I strayed the two-bed like an exile,
swallowing the scores of black sins
the fruit confessed. On the same day
(I was desolate, I moved quickly) I ordered a desk
from Amazon Prime; on the ninth I received
a single sturdier excuse for belonging
and scrawled your name along the courier's

dotted line. On the tenth day I danced with the vacuum
and spritzed myself with Windex, but the spiders
had untamed themselves and even the dust motes
sailed askance—at my desk I wrote to Sara
(*Yours faithfully, hairless and untailed,* I signed),
and the letters ran   wwwwwwwwwwild   with the know-
ldege taht   tehy cuold nwo   def-
ine   tiehr
prpoer
place.

On the twelfth day I beat down the asking price
of an olive branch and was escorted out
of Gerry's Garden Supply; I put the broken bough
to fertilize in a cornrow of hardwood where you
often nooked. I tallied a number of days and nights
before you even looked. On the *n*th day I fell over
myself searching for your favourite book—
angsty French play, all the characters feel stuck—
and plundering the shelf by the front window
glanced up; a bird we'd bred as an afterthought
(*dove*, to rhyme with your favourite word)
flew by, but when with two hands I permitted
the room to a sliver of sky there was only
a lone shred of laundry, fresh refugee
from the load of some other yard, some home
that someone else must pain to keep.

Self-Portrait with Virus

Those early spring mornings he
fed me salted butter and toasted
brioche, imported Japanese
tea; when he spoke, see,
it was as if Monet's water lilies
had waived their dimensions
to saturate my ears. My memory

hurts, my present is clogged.
I recline to horizontal, an amateur
fog. Vaguely I register that the plant
in my room has eaten almost all
its former shade of green; I picture
cooking something, but everything
feels raw, too graphic, pinch-pink.

DINNER SHIFT

There exist two types (deux types) *of people*
in this world, says Valentin, a knoll of cold
pizza in his mouth, all thin limb and chin
fuzz, wiggly roll of skin above his belt.
Those with the right to be happy, and those
without. I belong to the second kind.

We've hauled in the awnings, salvaged a few
sodden napkins from a further onslaught
of French rain; I'll never share in the same
language, so fall silent while he tucks in,
checks the forecast, the configurations
of the stars. *Cancer: neither love nor health*
bode well, he intones, chucking the paper
bin-ward with a mound of undercooked dough.

In drier weather, Sartre might have dined
here, left a good tip on the wine-begrimed
table and schlepped home to his feminist
manifestos, a warm fire—*The world makes*
more sense on a full stomach, claims Valentin,
but not much. He burps—*I find no reason*
to believe in women, or give up deep-
fried foods—and dips one hand into the tip
jar, then a plastic spoon into the last
tub of Grand Marnier chocolate mousse.

Lentilles

In French, the word for both lentils and contact lenses.

Sister, I watched you stir
a salt solution in the milky 9am light,
your hair darkly curtaining
the crystal-clear glass cups
that promised sight. And looking back
to your bare hands, your fingers lifting
the lentils of your contact lenses,
I close my eyes on infinite
tenderness: the image of you
rinsing your cymbals and fumbling
for vision after a night-tide of tears.
And if this is not the picture
of strength—you outfitting each
budding iris to meet the plastic
baptism of this new day—
I know no other. Maybe you do,
though. Maybe you will see beyond
the filtering panes of these few lines.

Debut

Midsummer. The air green, our skin
a practiced shade of brown. On the dock
a clutch of limbs, dimpled chests, fuller
dreams—Sadie presses her lips
to the drunken planks and draws back,
chafed, abstracted. I steal a kiss
from her glossed wand of watermelon
and wriggle in my throng of strings.
My mother, who has never worn
a bikini in her life, slipped me this
sliver of Lycra, a packet of Jujubes, two
disposable cameras. I hardly knew
how to step in, and the first day debuted
with the straps crossed all wrong.

The next morning at breakfast
Sadie's old man moves to undo a touch
of jelly from her upper lip
and draws back—she's been marked
overnight. In the canoe that afternoon
we ply the oars with Austin
from across the lake, and Sadie fingers
her *beauty spot*, flashes
a Cindy Crawford smile. I can hardly keep up,
my arms are so tired. We press on:
the sun dissolves, the loons cry out,
marshmallows soften near the fire. I suck
my sticky fingers and snap a photo of Sadie,
strange crown of flame around her face.

REBECCA LEVI

Ekstasis on Tremont Street

Rhonda's getting her roots
re-somethinged
That European therapist
says affairs are no one's fault

A truck of mirrors
cut up and stuck
on the wall in puzzle
pieces

It's America In the glass
Allison's foil blinks
crepe-paper light
I heard in India
people stay married

Dryers blowing scratchy

Nadja paints me
in a black bowl
I can feel it at the bottom
of my throat

Can dye seep inside?
Nadja's allergic
One time she did her own
hair and her head
pufferfished

Rinse
Neck nape
Ribbon cold

On the ceiling painted
stars no
constellations

Rhonda's balancing her checkbook
You know I hate
making generalizations
Her hair is frizzy like mine
but she's got kids
How do you all meet people?

I'm wrapped like
soft serve
earlobes dripping sugar
from the towel

I only get American girls
Nadja clacks
the dryer down
The American girls
they really go for me

Melt me golden
into palm
lines

Natick Center
Allison's got a nice new place
Walk-in closet Dryer static

When I run rivers
around myself
the best part is that I forget
to stop

Beatrice, Immaginata

Years scratching after her, that gold straw girl.
    Your Beatrice winked into the sun's
    long fringe, pink hoodie, pinker tongue uncurled.
Into the camera barefoot Bea lunged,
    her fingers splayed, anticipating you.
    She bought that scarf in Marrakech, in summer.
She bought it on the Po; I browse for truth
    in Bea's timeline snaps. I bet she liked
    a bracelet kiss on bone. She liked the fruit
your orchard grew. She hated Tuscan nights
    in camper vans; her skin was sand, her mouth
    a caramel you pocketed, wrapped tight.
You buy me peach gelato, lick me, cowed.
    La Bea moves the sun and other stars
    on foreign streets. This evening I'll allow
her climb up into me, her footsteps hard
    between my ribs. Her sugar breath. She peers
    out from my eyes. *So this is how it starts?*

Mikvah

For my grandmother, my great-grandmother, and my great-great-grandmother

Judith

Coney Island's Washington Baths— nearest I come
to a cleansing ritual. Sally and I go every day
in July, sweet sixteen, palming her family's season pass.
I close my eyes at the cool ink stamp, shiver
at goyish exclusivity, pull my lips
into my mouth. They make us shower first.
Bensonhurst sidewalk heat slides out from between
my thighs. In the pool, I sink, smile, feel the water
through my teeth. Open my eyes to let a little chlorine in.

Jeanne

We hitch from the Lower East Side. Almost
to Niagara. I dream the spray.
If I caught the falls in a bucket, how
much would it weigh? Could I run across
the drain? Ruthie won't move
on Shabbat. We're stuck in a motel in Buffalo.

Rivka

Her zich an Yudessel   Listen Judith I'll read to you
from the Women's Bible   God looked at
Adam wondering which organ   He should take

Not the eye   she'd see   not the ear
she'd hear   not the foot   she'd run
not the hand
                    she'd grasp

Arthritis

And now I only have the videos
you send. I back over the frames like tires

pack fresh earth. A glint of clavicle—
sweat slick? New season light? A chain you wear

I've already forgot? Comparing you
to broken glass would be too neat. My joints

ache. I tell myself I have arthritis—
a woman in my yoga class has some,

belied by hardest abs, bright flank tattoos.
Her chest heaves up, triumphant, rising clear

through full spine twists. Unblinks me in the mirror.

You're turning backward. Why do we have Fall
or Spring? Their names sloughed off, we'd pendulum

from heat to cold to heat. And twice a year,
we'd face-to-face the hesitation point.

October. I trick myself it's early spring.
Your valley lifts its head, rolls up the ice.

Your sun sits on its haunches, picks its teeth.

Appendix:

The world thins around me.
I never thought I'd miss the viscous.
Why does no one float here?
Even the fat pad who used to love me
slumps against the glass,
no good for conversation anymore.
The others never talked to me, unproductive slick of tissue,
useless and gorgeous—
isn't that the definition of art?
I let them worry about systems and viruses
(classic middle management)
and studied the greats.
Not Van Gogh or even Picasso;
I wanted south, post-colonial,
Kahlo and the Argentines
and of course Botero's bronze work—
naked giants with tiny genitals.
The large intestine rolled its eyes,
nothing new.
That's how I got into my Colombian period,
started puffing myself out.
I was trying voluminosity.
Pushing the envelope. Annoying the colon.
Only the fat pad appreciated
what I was doing,
so we hatched a plan to go live in Marfa
and make surrealist digital portraits
of very small things.
All I had to do was keep growing.
The fat pad elbowed out more space for me,
the intestines went crazy,
the colon flipped,
even the spleen heard about it.
We knew we'd be leaving soon.
Huddled together in the dark,
the fat pad stroked my inflamed back
and reminded me of our whys.

Now we’re in this glass house,
which isn’t how I pictured Marfa,
though let’s be honest it could be Marfa,
but just in case I keep an eye out for passing trucks
so we can hitch a ride to the desert.

ERIC HERTZ

Incarnation as Salt

Before he became a man, and healed
the sick, and died, and rose again, God

became salt. He was still waking up at dawn
when God yawned, raised his young arms up

above his head and let his grandmother slip
a crystal colored dress

over his formless face. What did God feel then
when the beasts stuck their pink tongues

on stones to taste him? People hungered, hacked,
gathered him up from black caves into fractured clumps

in sacks to sell. Inside the little glass churches on diner counters
he heard the endless debates of salts,

got swept up into their arguments,
cried out in their hunger and desire—

how they wanted to be baptized into water!
Some said dissolution would be only pain and further division.

Water, they said, was the scalpel that cleaved
the brain to make two minds

where one had been. They wanted it over and done,
like the souls of the damned that shake in craving,

eager to cross the Acheron into Hell.
Others contended water was Heaven's gate:

that dissolution was the rusting and crumbling of
a prison. The water's surface, they argued,

was the only wall between them and the one glassy God—
and that wall had no thickness.

God debated both positions,
remembered something, forgot it, forgot he'd ever

remembered, until the salt shaker shook,
and he slipped at last inside a bowl of soup.

Curled between its charge, he let the two parts
of his mind be pulled apart

but not quite divided—it was a gentle and natural
teasing, the way that sound divides into music

or hours sift into seconds. And then
he was no longer himself—he was other,

split and double, spinning. Two spoons
stirred his chloride and sodium parts—

two spoons of two lovers eating
together on a winter day: tomato bisque.

We can imagine in all horror
what it's like to die in crucifixion

but can we ever imagine what it's like
to fall into solution? To swell two lovers' bloods

thick, in swarms of cells—to be lost in life
as time is lost or caught inside a clock?

And yet, by God, we feel your fingers spinning around numbers
not our own, and feel our fingers sliding in return

to meet you there around a single spoon—
to meet you here—this sense-world, this soup, this spoon—this

is the only place we may feel your fractaled
face. So we do—we trace you, greedily, hesitantly,

and so, so tenderly. We drink you. We drink you
with the eye's dilation, and drink you with unclosable

ears, and squirrel tongues, and twitching horse's noses—
we know you though you've lost yourself too close.

You are the silent breath the singer takes before she sings.
Yes. That is the name I will settle for, for now.

But what in this name will she sing?

The Box in the Forest

Behind our apartment there was a little forested patch. That's where we found the cardboard box.

It didn't take long to learn what the box was for. If you went inside it, you would die.

We used to do it everyday after school. We'd make sure nobody else was around, then we'd crawl into the box and die.

We only ever died one at a time. If you were the mourner, sometimes you'd bang and wail on the box, or scream at the empty forest. Usually, you would just lean on the cardboard and stare out into the woods.

Then you'd lift the box up and switch places.

EVERY WORD IS A WELL

Every word is a well
into which a god fell
when gods walked the earth.

We grunt—pulling, pulling
at our knotted ropes,
but the cord's too weak to haul them up.

So they remain, curled up
in the dark circle of a syllable,
in the stone-lined throat.

Sometimes you can hear them
humming a tune from before
the time of words

or scratching out a picture
on the sides of the hole, and sometimes
if you listen closely

you can hear them yelp out to a crow
on the ledge, cawing back
in that old language. Usually though

the gods stay silent in their wells, save
for the creak and the splash
as they fill the pails we lower—

with what,
we do not know.
But I've heard it said

that if one sits quietly for long enough
with legs dangling over the wall,
breathing softly through the throat,

and expects nothing, expects
nothing at all, and even forgets about the word,
the throat, the breath, the god—then a ladder may appear

from below, and one may climb down
to meet the god at the bottom
of the silence of a word.

There are ancient paintings on the walls
of temple ruins, which depict
massive, weathered, six-fingered hands washing

human backs and necks
with the water of the stars.
What a relief, I imagine, it must be.

MORE VALUE OR MORE TIME?

On the screen of the New York City MetroCard machine appear two options:

MORE VALUE

or

MORE TIME?

More value or more time? That is a question you must answer if you would like to take the subway.

DANIEL HARDISTY

Bride

If I were to leave unannounced,
the band still playing in the wooded glade,
the drinks on tables and the bar wide open,

you're the one I'd take my cue from.
The way you slipped out the side door,
not even collecting your coat,

walking away from the marquee in winter
into the cold, scented air;
the dresses with their backs to you,

and the brightsided tent
becoming first a far-off cinema screen,
then a distant house with a single lit pane.

Siempre

Facing you,
I am not jealous.

If you arrived
with a man on your back,
or a hundred men
hanging in the rigging of your hair,
or a thousand men
sleeping on the soft mound of your belly,
if you were a river
filled with drowned men
met by the furious sea
foaming at its mouth,
by eternal weather –

if you arrived with them all
where I wait for you,
I would not be jealous.
We will always be alone.
We will always be, you and I,
alone on this earth
to begin life.

After Neruda

Radio

I tug the curtain to confirm
the weather I hear on the radio
the dark tear of a blackbird
against the untouched snow

THE FISH

Years after his death
my granddad announced his retirement
in a dream,

from here on in
he would spend his days at the pub;
half his money

would go to us,
and half his money to the *White Horse* till.
Why he told me this

after seven years
in the hardening ground, I don't know.
And why, in the dream,

after his long
declaration, he then changed into a fish
is hard to say.

A silver skinned fish
I duly wrapped in baking parchment
and tied with a bow.

Or *cooking paper*,
as I scribbled – when I first awoke – on the back
of an envelope.

MERMAID

On the third day she was still alive,
caked in healing salts.
her arms jeweled like peacock feathers.
Her shallow breathing gentle as the lapping
of water in a washbowl.
My cheap cotton towels wrung and re-soaked
and laid again along her dry tail,
the wire grill of scales
slowly finding their luster.

She slept.
I watched her like daft Narcissus in the pool.
Wiping the salt foam of her lips:
a silver fish flashed in the
black bowl of her eye.
She would live.

Swifts

The swifts arrive in Marfa, they will be through a few days and pass. They cover the power lines as if some spore has come to germination. Small crescent inquisitions that hang above, they examine me on the stoop. They want the ember in my cigarette and the secret of the gray breath my mouth exhales. They are gods of the little thunder; they might steal from me and slip back into their crowd.

In the courtyard white rinds of bark hang from the birches. Swifts fly amongst them, looping, landing, and revisiting their flights. They are planning something. The birches idle in the desert winds, their linen torn and falling. The cluttering birds are teasing them for their stiffness, their Southern manners, their old traditions. *Look: your time is done,* they say, *no husbands now are coming home.*

Libby Goss

Motions

On the 15th day,
half the moon closed her eye
and said:

I desire sunlight.
I desire a thousand waves
of radiation, a thousand cracks

to fill my bones, a light
that turns me blind and
cold I want a heat like sulfur.

I want a lover to hold beneath
the shape of the stars I
want a heath of comets,

a dusty evening, a ladder,
an ether shade to draw,
a bed that froths and curls.

I lack dreams. I have reveries,
none of them good. Everything
hooks before me in motion. Everything

circles in motion. I want
an explosion. A dark red that burns.
I want to shrivel, an ash over earth.

Edna Pontellier in Requiem

Drown,
down by the river,
one hand scraping for the sky.

Drown, a body
within the sand,
casting in the grainy night.

Drown, and all
the darkness swells
from the gaping of your eye.

Now the sea
foams. Now, the sea
is hot and bright.

Drown, and all her waves
are the gown, the veil
and pyre, the isle of light.

Midnight Corpus

In the night, I try
to move you,
your bones shifting

in the bed. What
kind of love
is this? — that I

would cross and
uncross your limbs
as though it mattered

in what angles they slept.
There, you breathe.
It is the racking

of a lung that barely
stands. Oh body,
oh corpus gaining

its evening. I take
your hand. The
dark and I grow.

To Mark Strand

I have eaten too
much of poetry.

My stomach swarms
with dogs. The

horses chew and
bray at my ears.

Even the orange
cuts my tongue.

Feed, beautiful sickness,
ifrit of the blood —

a dwelling for you
in this house of bone

cracking in the maws
of art.

I Picked Thee You Are Mine

I.

they buried her gray
body

an apple in her
hand

sleep now they said
softly

sleep now all is
eaten.

II.

i've come across two
ways

to say that i
am

sorry: one proffers an
orange

the other a bitten
apple

i've tried neither and
neither

says that i am
forgiven.

III.

at the sermon every
body

had an apple at
hand

the pews were filled
red

and every mouth watched
god.

Madeline Gilmore

The Brothers Lionheart

I. Stockholm

August. Dusk falling like something of a fog.

In our hotel there was a desk to write on—

I penned, Drink and be whole again beyond confusion.

So child-like when you sleep, you rose and saw the pad.

Me calling from the bath, "I'm so sorry,

you weren't meant to read that."

II. Stockholm

"They're going to colonize Mars," you said

over dinner—green pea sauce and fish lying in it—

though red dust doesn't appeal to us,

or, if it does, we're scared to admit it,

like the way you told me, "You are the best first love

I could have ever asked for." I imagine

Stockholm is beautiful in winter.

Dark, yes, and cold, and far away,

but nice, sometimes, to sleep,

and snow, and Christmas,

oh and don't forget—something about

the preciousness of hours.

III. Brooklyn

You call in October to say

there isn't a way you can do this anymore.

I haven't been myself.

One half is strewn between

the buildings and the sea.

The other is stuck in Stockholm

in midnight sun, where anyone

with a balcony can watch.

If I could remember when I was happy—

well, it's too near in the past—

vaguely, the shape of your arm

unfolding, the sound of your laugh.

IV. Stockholm

Outside the children's museum

the water was the water and there was

nothing about that,

and we had just seen two children die

two deaths each, those Brothers Lionheart

on the storybook ride. In the story,

the younger is ill, and the house catches fire.

The older holds the younger and jumps,

and from jumping, dies,

and if that wasn't already too much

for a children's ride, the younger's

illness overcomes him.

They meet in a new world

wherein there are battles to be fought

and grass (an oversight on the part

of the museum staff, I think).

Outside, I saw you, and I was mad,

saying, "Who would ever write a story like that?"

asking all the wrong questions,

aggregate, ever.

V. Brooklyn

November's got me thinking again about the freedom of form,

the things we say to justify our lives.

November in the house of the child I watch for money.

I don't know where you are.

"My aunt has died," I tell the child,

who has refused to eat his dinner and is writhing

beneath the table, laughing and kicking up his legs.

"My aunt has died, can you please get off the floor."

We go to the roof for something to do.

Cars flow over a bridge from both directions,

people emerge from basements of attorneys at law,

and the feral cats wander around the wharfs.

Somewhere there's a place my size,

a good view of a chapel tower and a slice of trees,

or even just a leaf. I don't ask

for much. I ask for

one red petal, that's all.

VI. Stockholm

In the light-filled stair you hugged me

and sent me to bed, and the hotel sent me soup

and fresh baked bread. Later,

the beach. We walked to the end

where the sand dropped off in a cliff.

It is useful to feel small, even against water.

The Brothers Lionheart were confronted

with a dragon in a great ravine.

They were fighters—they were

tethered together by something.

In the end, the younger takes the older,

fatally burned by dragon's fire,

onto his back and jumps into the ravine

to the brink of some other death,

meaning, you are a good brother,

meaning, you have raised me,

meaning, accept my life,

accept my life.

VII. Brooklyn

I don't want to be so thin but there doesn't seem to be

a way to add weight.

I had an awful vision: not myself hanging,

but I saw the rope, and it was beautifully threaded,

gilt and grey as breath when it becomes smoke.

The Christmas trees are piled all throughout the city,

overwhelming the usual smells with pine,

with the time it takes to unstick

from a base and fall in a heap.

It is a lovely green, with brown beneath,

drying and by Valentine's, I'm sure, demolished.

VIII. Brooklyn

You know, this is the nicest street in Brooklyn,

and the house I'd pick

is the white one, with the trellis

and the latticed window shades.

Down the street comes a shout—

"Someone call the police!"

That's the rule of the human mind, you'd say.

That's the rule, no one will call.

So the children died, and died.

Whoever was supposed to take care of them

went to see the house destroyed by fire.

IX. Stockholm

In some manner we were going to be moved—

seated in the chair with you,

your sisters in the other, your mother.

After all, it was a ride.

X. Brooklyn

"Is this the nether mead?"

a child asks me in the park.

"I don't know," I say.

To me it looks like the meadow.

"Not the meadow," she says,

"That's the other one."

She runs to catch a falling leaf.

I lie on my back and watch

the small hawks circling the trees.

Do you know where I am now?

In the meadow, or the nether mead.

Anyway, somewhere in the grass.

An Afterword by Robert Pinsky

A group of people can develop a personality of its own, quite separate from each person, unpredictably distinct from any of the individuals and generated by all of them. Teachers know this. We may find one class to be cheery, while another is depressive. One overall personality may be sullen but brilliant, while another is kind of the opposite— co-operative but bumbling. These various adjectives, as with individuals, merely gesture toward the complicated, shifting nature of an actual, breathing whole.

This collection of poems demonstrates that a group can also be remarkably creative, enormously imaginative—a quality that arises not from unanimity but from its opposite. The pronounced, even idiosyncratic differences among these eight young poets have manifested an unusual, engaging whole. All of us who know them agree that they are remarkably gifted as well as consistently generous with one another and with the world. The group is confident enough to produce this collection, with that confidence based in a shared understanding that as artists they are gifted in various, fluid ways.

So, it is like the glancing, reflective wit of this gestalt personality to begin a book with a poem entitled "Tabula Rasa" (p.3). That is, this collection from a writing program opens with the idea of the blank page. And on the other hand, the speed and insouciance of the poem is distinctly like Emily Yaremchuk and no one else:

I'm wild for heirlooms. The cold jacket
of an old bullet fits snug in my cheek.
It is easy to become you among these things.

In the second drawer, I unearth
your marriage license and faded pornography
beneath a phalanx of rolled socks.

I'm your daughter. I can disappear entirely
in a rack of your suits. I cut the daffodils
out front before they are done growing,

fix their waxy stems between my fingers
like puppeteer's bars. I piss in the yard
like I am God.

This passage from the middle of Yaremchuk's poem in a characteristic way swerves happily from the implicit to the explicit "I'm your daughter."

A quite different flavor of the explicit and a quite different other-person characterize Kathleen Radigan's "The Kitchen Staff at Ocean World Bar & Grille." (p.18) Unlike some of Radigan's work this might be called "narrative," but in a sense that is turbo-charged by her terrific way with dialogue, and with her knowing, effective play been strong verbs (e.g. "slides," "clocks out," "swish") and strong, verb-less sentence fragments:

She says she would've been
an astronaut but her vision
is shit so it's fine she got
knocked up. I say I'm sad
about a man. She says,
"Men are liars." (Once she found
her friend dead, stabbed
in a bathroom. Three kids
crying in a locked closet.)

She flips patties, smiles side-eyed
at the griddle,
slides me a ham sandwich.
Her girls are 7 and 4.
She boils them hot dogs
after each shift, toasts the buns.
She says they're going
to the public pool tomorrow.
She says, "Don't think
you'll never find someone

because we've all felt
like that and we all found someone."

Then clocks out. Double
doors swish behind her. Soap
bubbles on her T-shirt. Drowning
she swims with a riptide. Spat up
from the ocean.

That closing series of short units, to my ear, has the effect of honoring the character's autonomous, layered and mysterious being: wonder, the opposite of condescension.

More expressionistic, with a more thrashing eloquence, Lauren Peat's "Postscript" (p.23) delights in something like a collision between the ordinary and the mythological, two modes locked in mutual need and mistrust, laughter and calamity, a sort of Biblical domestic comedy:

On the twelfth day I beat down the asking price
of an olive branch and was escorted out
of Gerry's Garden Supply; I put the broken bough
to fertilize in a cornrow of hardwood where you
often nooked. I tallied a number of days and nights
before you even looked. On the n*th day I fell over*
myself searching for your favourite book—
angsty French play, all the characters feel stuck—
and plundering the shelf by the front window
glanced up; a bird we'd bred as an afterthought
(dove, *to rhyme with your favorite word)*
flew by, but when with two hands I permitted
the room to a sliver of sky there was only
a lone shred of laundry, fresh refugee
from the load of some other yard, some home
that someone else must pain to keep.

Peat attains an effective variation of the idea proposed by Elizabeth Bishop and others: the more fantastical the material, the more matter-of fact the narration. In this workaday fable, both kinds of material are set forth by a voice that is double: reportorial in tone, fabular in narrative structure.

In another kind of spectacular imagination-show, Rebecca Levi's "Appendix" (p.36) is spoken by . . . an appendix. This organ, contained in glass, knows art history and has emotional attachments. The sense of conviction gives this dramatic monologue pathos as well as comedy, from the opening "The world thins/ around me. I never thought/ I'd miss the viscous."

I'll quote the second half of the poem, to show what I mean: the pathos of limited perspective, played against longing, is universal, and the ridiculous premise emphasizes that:

The large intestine rolled its eyes,
nothing new.
That's how I got into my Colombian period,
started puffing myself out.
I was trying voluminosity.
Pushing the envelope. Annoying the colon.
Only the fat pad appreciated
what I was doing,
so we hatched a plan to go live in Marfa
and make surrealist digital portraits
of very small things.
All I had to do was keep growing.
The fat pad elbowed out more space for me,
the intestines went crazy,
the colon flipped,
even the spleen heard about it.
We knew we'd be leaving soon.
Huddled together in the dark,
the fat pad stroked my inflamed back
and reminded me of our whys.
Now we're in this glass house,
which isn't how I pictured Marfa,
though let's be honest it could be Marfa,
but just in case I keep an eye out for passing trucks
so we can hitch a ride to the desert.

The personal, here too, is also social.

That observation about Rebecca Levi's poem suggests some of what these eight poets have in common. I'll express it by quoting (without attribution) a memorable nasty remark someone I know made about an eminent, much-admired poet (to remain anonymous): "He writes very well about his little feelings." That bit of snark does not apply here; these young poets look out at the world.

For example, Eric Hertz's compact, penetrating "The Box in the Forest" (p.44), with its telling first-person plural, orchestrated in relation to the second-person singular, seems to be about death but effectively considers imagination as simultaneously communal and personal, individual and cultural:

Behind our apartment there was a little forested patch. That's where we found the cardboard box.

It didn't take long to learn what the box was for. If you went inside it, you would die.

We used to do it everyday after school. We'd make sure nobody else was around, then we'd crawl into the box and die.

We only ever died one at a time. If you were the mourner, sometimes you'd bang and wail on the box, or scream at the empty forest. Usually, you would just lean on the cardboard and stare out into the woods.

Then you'd lift the box up and switch places.

"We only ever died one at a time" is a well-made, writerly sentence. It also defines the imaginative game, crucially, as it involves what "we" experience together and also "one at a time."

It's worth observing that this group of poets, in their different ways, also share a ready, adaptable formal mastery: a prose poem, blank verse, a diagram, columns, tercets, whatever, might come from any one of them. Like Hertz, Daniel Hardisty has written good prose poems. He also knows how to make varying, short free verse lines dance with sentences (p.54):

THE FISH

Years after his death
my granddad announced his retirement
in a dream,

from here on in
he would spend his days at the pub;
half his money

would go to us,
and half his money to the White Horse *till.*
Why he told me this

after seven years
in the hardening ground, I don't know.
And why, in the dream,

after his long
declaration, he then changed into a fish
is hard to say.

A silver skinned fish
I duly wrapped in baking parchment
and tied with a bow.

Or cooking paper,
as I scribbled – when I first awoke – on the back
of an envelope.

I admire not only the rhythms, moments like the propulsive enjambment on "after his long/ declaration," but also the shrewd, touching syntactical placements: the sentence fragment that resists making "A silver skinned fish" the subject of a verb, "I don't know" at the end of that sentence beginning with "why." These matters of harmony and melody give the emotion its breath and its bite.

In Libby Goss's "Motions" (p.59), the opening resembles the fable-mode I've quoted from Lauren Peat, with that opening note of similarity highlighting the difference. Goss doesn't mix the intensity with a shopping trip; she takes it simultaneously inward and upward, as "half the moon closed her eye/ and said":

I desire sunlight.
I desire a thousand waves
of radiation, a thousand cracks

to fill my bones, a light
that turns me blind and
cold I want a heat like sulfur.

I want a lover to hold beneath
the shape of the stars I
want a heath of comets,

a dusty evening, a ladder,
an ether shade to draw,
a bed that froths and curls.

I lack dreams. I have reveries,
none of them good. Everything
hooks before me in motion. Everything

circles in motion. I want
an explosion. A dark red that burns.
I want to shrivel, an ash over earth.

Here, Goss's way of counterposing the anaphora on "I" with the varying rhythm of the lines, provides another example of how these poets take differing approaches to formal possibilities—while sharing a lively alertness to formal possibilities.

For example, Madeline Gilmore's poem in sections, "The Brothers Lionheart," deploys the spatial subtitles "Brooklyn" and "Stockholm" as temporal markers, the two places as (respectively) indicating "then" and "now." That lucid formal structure gets winningly, subtly countered by a shifty, expansive, syncopated point of view, as in "IV. Stockholm" (pp.69-70):

Outside the children's museum

the water was the water and there was

nothing about that,

and we had just seen two children die

two deaths each, those Brothers Lionheart

on the storybook ride. In the story,

the younger is ill, and the house catches fire.

The older holds the younger and jumps,

and from jumping, dies,

and if that wasn't already too much

for a children's ride, the younger's

illness overcomes him.

They meet in a new world

wherein there are battles to be fought

and grass (an oversight on the part

of the museum staff, I think).

Outside, I saw you, and I was mad,

saying, "Who would ever write a story like that?"

asking all the wrong questions,

aggregate, ever.

By "syncopated" I mean touches like the oddball word "aggregate," a noun in adjectival clothing (or is it the other way around?) suggesting the first-person's impulse to fit unlike things together, including times and ("ever") places. Like "there was/ nothing about that," "aggregate" suggests a personal, inward voice complicating and subverting the orderly, note-taking falsehood of straight-ahead narrative.

In summary: this book offers a pleasing, authentic variety of poets who share poetry's happy, stringent disregard for conventions and clichés: form as a truth-detector. I'm grateful to know these poets and their work.

About the Poets

A native of Fairfax, Virginia, **Emily Yaremchuk** is an alumna of the University of Virginia, where she earned a Bachelor of Arts degree with high distinction in English and anthropology and participated in the Area Program in Poetry Writing. An avid fan of punk music and all things English, she aspires to live in London's West End...or somewhere thereabouts. Her poems have appeared in publications such as *The Turnip Truck(s)*, the *Virginia Literary Review*, and *The Merrimack Review*, among others. She was recently awarded second-place in the 2017 Mick Imlah Poetry Prize for her poem "Tabula Rasa."

Kathleen Radigan is a native Rhode Islander. She graduated from Wesleyan University in 2017 with an English major and a psychology minor. She dabbled in theater and singing in college, worked at a preschool and in an infant language learning lab, and won the English Department's Sophie and Anne Reed and Sarah Hannah prizes for poetry. Wesleyan also awarded her an Olin Fellowship to study banshees and other ghosts in Ireland. Her poems can be found on the The Academy of American Poets website and PANK blog and in *The Adroit Journal*, *The Merrimack Review*, *The Harpoon Review*, *Maudlin House*, *Hermeneutic Chaos Literary Journal*, and a few others.

Born in Boston, Massachusetts, **Lauren Peat** was raised in the English Midlands and the various boroughs of Toronto. An intermittent teacher, translator, and editor, she swears by Joni Mitchell's principle of creative "crop rotation": she has toured internationally with a competitive chamber choir, contributed libretti to original vocal compositions, and performed spoken word in Bordeaux, Paris, and Provence, France. Her favourite Joni Mitchell song is "A Case of You."

Rebecca Levi is a musician, poet, and translator. Originally from New York City, she graduated from Yale University in 2007 and since then has lived in Peru, Colombia, and the U.S. Her work has appeared in *Columbia Journal*, *No Tokens Journal*, *Your Impossible Voice*, *BorderSenses*, and with Princeton University Press. Her translations of Chilean poet Stella Díaz Varín won second place in the Robert Fitzgerald Translation Prize at Boston University, and her poem about pigs and break-ups, "December 31st," won third place in the 2018 Mick Imlah Poetry Prize at *The Times Literary Supplement*. Rebecca's band is called Debarro, meaning "of mud" and ever-changing, which also describes what she likes about poetry.

Eric Hertz has a B.A. in philosophy and religious studies from Stanford University and grew up in New Jersey before moving out to the West Coast. He wrote and published a collection of poetry, *At the Park*, through the Stanford Honors in the Arts Program; the book explores an imagined world of strange games. Eric likes to write at the intersections of eastern philosophy, psychoanalysis, mythology, religious ritual, and ecology.

Daniel Hardisty was born in the U.K. He studied English and creative writing at the University of East Anglia. His poems have appeared in *Poetry London*, *Poetry Ireland Review*, *The Rialto*, *Poetry Salzburg Review*, *The Spectator*, *The Dark Horse*, and elsewhere, as well as on the BBC. He has received an Arts Council award from Arts Council England and a New Writing North Award and was highly commended in the Faber New Poets competition in 2014. He became a joint U.S. and U.K. citizen in 2015.

Libby Goss grew up in Stow, Massachusetts. She holds a B.A. from New York University Gallatin in creative writing, marketing, and publishing. She is interested in narrative and blurring the border between poetry and fiction and spends most of her free time running and listening to music from the 90s.

Born and raised in North Carolina, **Madeline Gilmore** moved to Brooklyn after receiving a Hubbard Hutchinson Memorial Fellowship from Williams College in 2015. In New York, she received a Brooklyn Poets fellowship, which helped inspire the long poem that appears in this anthology. Her poetry has appeared in *Bluestem* magazine and *The New Guard*, as well as *Massachusetts's Best Emerging Poets* anthology. Madeline doesn't know exactly what she'll be up to in the coming years, but she hopes she gets some good poetry out of them.

if you're not happy now